Will and Orv

by Walter A. Schulz
illustrations by Janet Schulz

On My Own
HISTORY
Grades 2-3

Carolrhoda Books, Inc./Minneapolis

For Cheryl McHenry,
a friend to children and books,
and a friend to us.

This book is available in two editions:
Library binding by Carolrhoda Books, Inc.
Soft cover by First Avenue Editions
Divisions of Lerner Publishing Group
241 First Avenue North
Minneapolis, MN 55401 U.S.A.

Website address: www.lernerbooks.com

Library of Congress Cataloging-in-Publication Data

Schulz, Walter A.
　Will and Orv / by Walter A. Schulz; illustrations by Janet Schulz.

　　p. cm—(A Carolrhoda on my own book)
　Summary: On a windy day in Kitty Hawk, N.C. in 1903, the
Wright brothers attempt to make history as they prepare the
''Flyer'' for the world's first engine-powered flight.
　ISBN 0-87614-669-8 (lib. bdg.)
　ISBN 0-87614-568-3 (pbk.)
　1. Wright, Orville, 1871-1948—Juvenile literature. 2.
Wright, Wilbur, 1867-1912—Juvenile literature. 3.
Aeronautics—History—United States—Juvenile literature.
[1. Wright, Orville, 1871-1948, 2. Wright, Wilbur, 1867-
1912. 3. Aeronautics—Biography.] I. Schulz, Janet, ill.
II. Title. III. Series: Carolrhoda on my own books.
TL540.W7S38　1991
629.13'0092'2—dc20　　　　　　　　　　　　　　91-9637
[B]

Manufactured in the United States of America
7 8 9 10 11 12 – JR – 05 04 03 02 01 00

Author's Note

The events that took place on December 17, 1903, when Wilbur and Orville Wright first flew an aircraft with a motor, changed the history of the world. The Wright brothers made many parts of their flying machine at their bicycle shop in Dayton, Ohio. Then they tested their ideas on the sand dunes of Kitty Hawk, North Carolina. They soon showed people how to fly like birds.

Until Wilbur and Orville brought together the necessary ideas, no one in history had ever built a machine that could take off from level ground and fly. The brothers did not invent human flight, but they developed the method to enable the first engine-powered aircraft to go up, down, and turn. Wilbur and Orville hand-made all the parts, including the propeller, and even built the engine for the craft they named *Flyer*.

Will and Orv is based on historical records of that windy December day long ago. The words spoken by the characters in the story were invented by the author to bring life to the event. There were five people who witnessed the first flight of the *Flyer*—four men were from the nearby life-saving station, and the other is identified as "young Johnny Moore of Nag's Head."

Johnny Moore looked out the window.
Gray winter clouds filled the sky.
The wind was blowing so hard
that the roof shook.

"Be no fishing today,"
his mother said.
Johnny groaned to himself.
Another slow day of fixing
fishnets and doing chores.
His mother smiled.
"How about bringing some fish
to the men at the life-saving
station?" she asked.

Johnny jumped up.
"I'll be back early!"
He put on his coat.
Then he ran along the beach.
Big waves crashed upon the shore.

Johnny lived on one of the
sandy islands off North Carolina
called the Outer Banks.
The islands could be very dangerous.
Every year, bad weather wrecked
many of the ships that passed by.

The people at the life-saving
stations rescued many sailors
from sinking ships.
Johnny liked to visit the brave men
who lived at the station close to
the village of Kitty Hawk.

But most of all, he liked
to watch the Wright brothers,
Wilbur and Orville.
The brothers lived at the
bottom of a big hill near
the life-saving station.
They flew down the hill
on big gliders.

For three summers,
Will and Orv had come
to North Carolina from Ohio.
They said that the Outer Banks
were dangerous for ships.
But they were the best place
to test their gliders,
machines that flew on the wind.

The wind blew every day.
The sand was soft.
There were no trees
or rocks to run into!

Many people in the nearby villages
thought Will and Orv were crazy.
Johnny thought they were very smart.
Once Johnny heard people
talking about Will and Orv.
Johnny told them, "I saw Will
fly down the hill just like a bird!"
One of the women said,
"A bird can fly wherever it wants.
A bird can fly right off the ground.
It doesn't need a hill to jump off."
They all laughed except Johnny.

Once, Johnny saw the strangest thing
when he visited Will and Orv.
The brothers were putting
a motor on a big glider.
They called this glider
a flying machine.
They named it *Flyer*.

This year Will and Orv hadn't gone
home at the end of the summer.
They stayed so that they
could test the *Flyer*.
Will and Orv told Johnny that no one
had ever flown into the sky
using a motor on a flying machine.

Just the thought of flying
made Johnny's heart thump.
Going down the hill
on a glider was exciting.
But flying up
with the birds was scary.
What if the motor stopped?
Or one of the wings broke?

The wind was still blowing
when Johnny reached
the life-saving station.
He opened the door.
"Hello, Johnny," said Mr. Daniels.
"I see you've brought
us some fish."
Johnny sat at the long table.

"The other day Will and Orv
tried to fly their machine,"
Mr. Daniels said.
"You mean the one with
the motor?" asked Johnny.
"Yup," he said. "But it didn't work.
The machine made a big bounce
and then smacked into the sand."

"Those propellers were spinning fast.
You can't even
see them turning!" said Mr. Daniels.
"Propellers?" Johnny asked.
"The motor turns
two big spinning blades.
They push the glider up
into the sky," said Mr. Daniels.

Johnny was amazed.

"Will and Orv must be the bravest
people in the world!" said Johnny.

"That's for sure.

Other people tried the same thing
with a flying machine.

But it crashed right into a river,"
Mr. Daniels said as he shook his head.

Just then they heard a voice yell
from the lookout tower.
Mr. Westcott called down,
"The flag is up!
Will and Orv are going to try out
their flying machine again!"

Johnny jumped up from the table.

He knew the flag was a signal.

It meant that the brothers needed help

with one of their machines.

Four of the men left quickly.

Johnny ran to keep up.

As they reached the first shed,
Orv came out.
He had on a stiff collar and a tie.
The brothers always dressed up.
"Hello, boys," Orv said.
"Great day for flying."

One of the men answered,
"The wind is blowing too hard.
It's a great day for
breaking your neck!"
"We can't wait any longer," Orv said.
"The weather is turning bad.
We're already months late
in testing the *Flyer*."

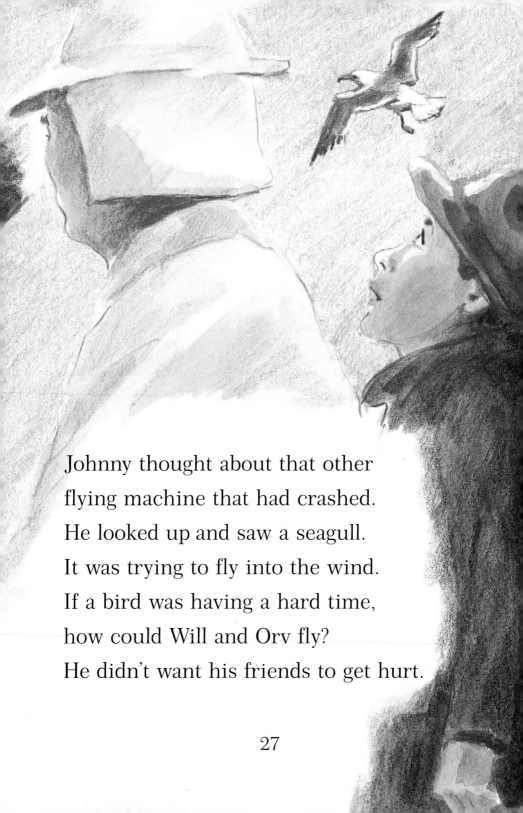

Johnny thought about that other
flying machine that had crashed.
He looked up and saw a seagull.
It was trying to fly into the wind.
If a bird was having a hard time,
how could Will and Orv fly?
He didn't want his friends to get hurt.

27

Will came out of the shed.
"The wind is blowing hard—
more than 25 miles an hour,
Orv," he said.
He looked very worried.
Orv looked up at the gray sky.
"This is our day, Will.
Today is our day
to finally fly!" said Orv.
He opened the big doors
on the second shed.
Inside in the dark sat the *Flyer*.
It was much bigger
than the gliders.
But the flying machine
didn't look very strong.
The *Flyer* seemed to be made
of matchsticks and cloth.

Johnny saw the motor
on the bottom wing.
The two propellers
were behind the wings.

Will climbed onto the *Flyer*.
He lay down on his stomach
on a flat piece of wood.
He was right next to the motor.
Will moved around
until he was comfortable.
Wires leading to the wings were
attached to the boards he was lying on.
When Will moved the boards
from side to side, the wings twisted
and changed shape.

"This is the secret to flying,
Johnny," Will said.
"Other people have flown on gliders.
But this flying machine
can change directions.
Whenever I move, the wings
twist just like a bird's."

Orv turned to Johnny.

"Look at the motor we built," he said.

"It's as strong as eight horses."

Johnny was speechless.

He didn't believe that

the little engine could be

as powerful as even one horse.

Will climbed off the *Flyer*.

"We're ready.

Let's put the track down," he said.

They carried out smooth pieces of wood.

Then they placed them end to end

to make a track.

The *Flyer* had no wheels.

It had runners like a sled

so it wouldn't sink in the soft sand.

Johnny helped hold
the *Flyer* on the track.
The wind almost lifted it up.
Johnny and the others held on
with all their might.

Orv climbed onto the machine.
He lay down on the wood
near the middle of the wing.
He turned his hat around
so it wouldn't blow off.

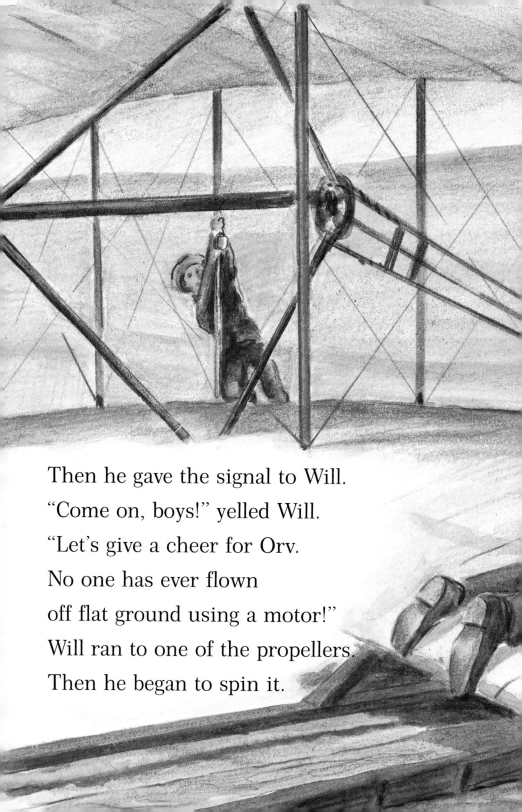

Then he gave the signal to Will.

"Come on, boys!" yelled Will.

"Let's give a cheer for Orv.

No one has ever flown

off flat ground using a motor!"

Will ran to one of the propellers.

Then he began to spin it.

"R-R-R-R," the motor
started with a loud roar.
Johnny jumped at the noise.
Black smoke shot out of a pipe.
The *Flyer* started to shake.
It seemed about to fall apart.

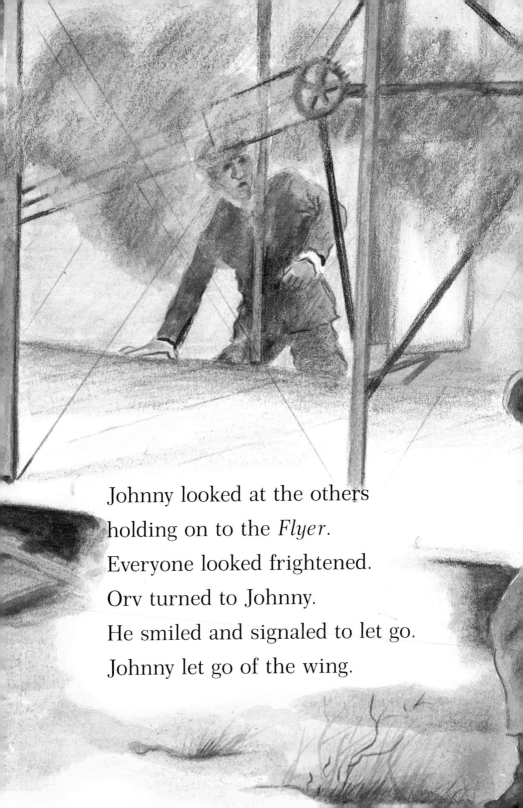

Johnny looked at the others
holding on to the *Flyer*.
Everyone looked frightened.
Orv turned to Johnny.
He smiled and signaled to let go.
Johnny let go of the wing.

Orv let loose the wire
that held the machine to the track.
The *Flyer* started to move slowly.
Will held one wing and started
to walk along with the *Flyer*.
Soon he was running.
The *Flyer* quickly picked up speed.
Will finally let go.
"IT'S UP!"
The *Flyer* lifted up off the track.

It flew right into the wind.
The flying machine rose up
and then plunged down into the sand.
Johnny was scared.
Everyone began to run.

Orv lay very still on the wing.

The motor was running.

The propellers continued to spin.

"Orv, are you all right?" yelled Will.

No answer.

Finally Orv moved.

He reached over

and turned the motor off.

Slowly, he stood up.

Orv stepped down onto the ground.

He brushed the sand from his face.

"I guess we sure flew today, Will.

How long was the flight?"

Orv said with a big smile.

"Twelve seconds. And over 120 feet!"

shouted Will.

The two brothers happily shook hands.

Will turned to the helpers and said,

"You are the official witnesses

to the first powered flight.

A flying machine with a person on it

took off on its own power.

And it flew under control!"

Orv looked at Johnny.
"What you saw has
never been done before.
We are the first.
We couldn't have done it
without help from you and the others.
Always remember December 17, 1903."